I enjoyed making this & I hope you enjoy it too!

Love, Anna x

Thank you

To Mum and Dad for helping me,

To little Sis, you busy bee,

To Anca, who you will agree

Has done the pictures brilliantly.

ELGA PRESS

www.elgapress.co.uk

First published UK, 2021 by Elga Press
ISBN 978-1-915119-00-1

Graphic Designer: Mihai Ene
Text Editor: Tania Barlow

Ned, Ned,
Bed, Bed, Bed!

written by

Anna MacBain

illustrated by

Anca Chelaru

I wonder if you can:

- Find Coco the hamster hiding on each page
- Tell someone what Lola the cat thinks about Ned
- Think of your own reasons why bed is good for Ned

One day my daddy said to me,

"You're tired, my boy, don't you agree?

Oh Ned! Oh Ned!

It's time for you to go to bed!"

So I asked the kitchen-maid,
"Please rescue me from my bed."
"Oh Ned! Oh Ned!" she softly said,
"It's time for you to go to bed!"

Next, I told my dear mummy,

"Come here right now and cuddle me."

"My precious boy, oh darling Ned,

It's time for you to go to bed!"

After that, I dared to hope.
I said to Sis, “I just can’t cope,
I need your help, if not, I’ll yelp!”
“Oh, Neddy, Ned!” my sister said,
“It’s time for you to go to bed!”

So then I asked our baby Ted,

“Can you please save me from my bed?”

He clapped his hands and sweetly said,

”Ned, Ned, bed, bed, bed!”

I went outside and begged the guy,
The gardener who's passing by,
"The sun's still up, it's not yet time,
For me to have my beddy-byes."

The gardener smiled and replied,
"When I was a lad and I had lied,
I was sent to bed for hours,
Unable to tend to my flowers."

"They tried to stop me being rude,
And it forever cured my mood.
Oh Ned! Oh Ned!" the gardener said,
"It's time for you to go to bed!"

"Oh, who is smart and who is wise?"
I searched low, and I looked high.
I shouted, "I've got an idea!
I'll go to my garden over here."

"Of course, the owl!" I cry.
"You are the wise one, sir, oh my!
The teacher says you are clever.
If you help me, I won't pluck a feather!"

The owl replied,
With peaceful eyes,
"I want to test the evening breeze.
So I'm awake, but should you be?"

"Be wise and let the dreams take you,
To lands afar, adventures new.
Oh Ned! Oh Ned!" the owl said,
"It's time for you to go to bed!"

What else to do, but turn around?
Without a word, without a sound.
I see Queenie hanging on the wall,
In the centre of our hall.

I tell her Majesty's painting,
"You've got a very high rating.
If someone can help, you can.
Sleeping I would like to ban!"

"Please help me,
Oh my Queen,
Don't be cruel,
Don't be mean!"

She stares at me as if to say,

“Master Ned, off on your way.

Can’t you see? I would quite like my tea!

Oh Ned, oh Ned, it’s time for you to go to bed!”

I stomped to my bedroom,
To shake off the gloom,
And grabbed good old bear,
My loving friend, who's always there.

"Oh, furry ball of fluff,
Save me, or I'll huff and puff.
I cannot enter a silly bed,
Or I may just lose my head."

Bear, fat and plump, sitting flat on his rump.
Grumpy and cross, he was not my boss.
He might as well have said,
"Oh Ned! Oh Ned! It's time for you to go to bed!"

And now I dared to ask the mite,
The hamster in the cage who BITES.
"You're the last hope to get me out.
I know you can, there is no doubt."

And then I heard him sneakily say,
"Come in, my boy, come share my cage."
That surely gave me quite a fright,
I answered, in a jiffy, alright.

"I'm so sorry, please don't bite,
I think my loving folks are right.
It's time for me to say...
Good Night!"

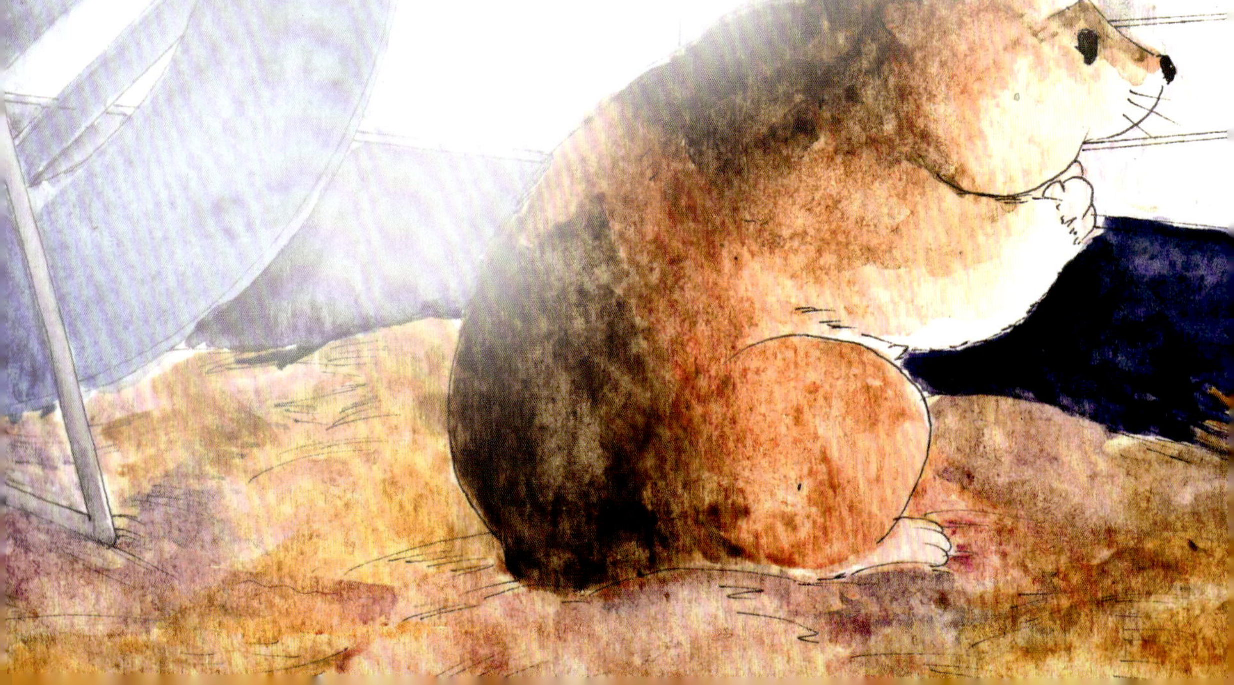

Night, night, sleep tight!